I0815765

ENGINEERING ANSWERS

How Bridges Stand Strong

BY JOANNE MATTERN

An Imprint of Abdo Publishing
abdobooks.com

abdobooks.com

Printed in the United States of America, North Mankato, Minnesota.
102024
012025

Cover Photo: Simon Lukas/Shutterstock Images
Interior Photos: Shutterstock Images, 4–5, 15, 16, 24, 28; Juan Carlos Alonso Lopez/Shutterstock Images, 6; Ale Argentieri/Shutterstock Images, 8; Creative Family/Shutterstock Images, 10–11; hpbfotos/Alamy, 13; Underwood Archives/Archive Photos/Getty Images, 18–19; Xiong Qi/Xinhua News Agency/Getty Images, 20; Denise Sarlin/Gamma-Rapho/Getty Images, 22; Costfoto/Future Publishing/Getty Images, 25; Richard Semik/Shutterstock Images, 26; Chuangxin Zhou/Shutterstock Images, 29 (top); Mariusz Bugno/Shutterstock Images, 29 (bottom)

Editor: Marley Richmond
Series Designer: Laura Kuchar

Library of Congress Control Number: 2024938354

Publisher's Cataloging-in-Publication Data

Names: Mattern, Joanne, author.
Title: How bridges stand strong / by Joanne Mattern
Description: Minneapolis, Minnesota: ABDO Publishing, 2025 | Series: Engineering answers | Includes online resources and index.
Identifiers: ISBN 9781098295851 (lib. bdg.) | ISBN 9798384916857 (ebook)
Subjects: LCSH: Engineering--Juvenile literature. | Bridges--Juvenile literature. | Bridge construction industry--Juvenile literature. | Design-build process (Construction industry)--Juvenile literature. | Questions and answers--Juvenile literature. | Engineering design--Juvenile literature.
Classification: DDC 620.1--dc23

CONTENTS

Tower Bridge is named after the Tower of London, which stands nearby.

CHAPTER 1

Raising the Bridge

A car drives through the crowded streets of London, the United Kingdom. It is heading toward Tower Bridge, which crosses the River Thames. The bridge has stood in London for more than 130 years. Thousands of people and cars cross it every day.

There are two walkways high above the main roadway of Tower Bridge. People need tickets to cross these walkways.

As the car approaches the bridge, traffic lights turn red. Cars and people have to wait to cross the bridge. A large ship is heading up the river. It is about to go under the bridge. But the ship is too tall to pass under the roadway. So the roadway has to move.

The ship gets closer. Four bolts that hold the roadway together slide back. Machines called bascules on the ends of the bridge rotate. The movement causes the two halves of the bridge to lift up in the middle. Drivers and pedestrians watch as the bridge opens. The ship easily passes through.

The bascules then reverse. The roadway comes down. The bolts reconnect. The lights turn green. The bridge is ready for cars and people to travel across it again.

From Steam to Electricity

Originally, the bascules on Tower Bridge were powered by steam. Eventually, it became too expensive to keep the steam engine running. So the bascule system switched to electricity. This power source is less costly and more practical.

Pons Fabricius is an ancient bridge in Italy. It was built more than 2,000 years ago and still stands strong today.

What Is a Bridge?

A bridge is a structure that goes over an obstacle. Sometimes the obstacle is water. Sometimes it is a valley. Other bridges cross over highways or train tracks. People have used bridges to get from one place to another since ancient times.

A bridge can be as simple as a log over a stream. Or it can be a complex structure made of steel, concrete, and cables that **spans** many miles. Modern bridges use science and math in many ways to cross a wide range of gaps.

Explore Online

Visit the website below. Does it give more information about the topic in Chapter One?

Amazing Hydraulics: The Story of Tower Bridge, London

abdocorelibrary.com/bridges-stand-strong

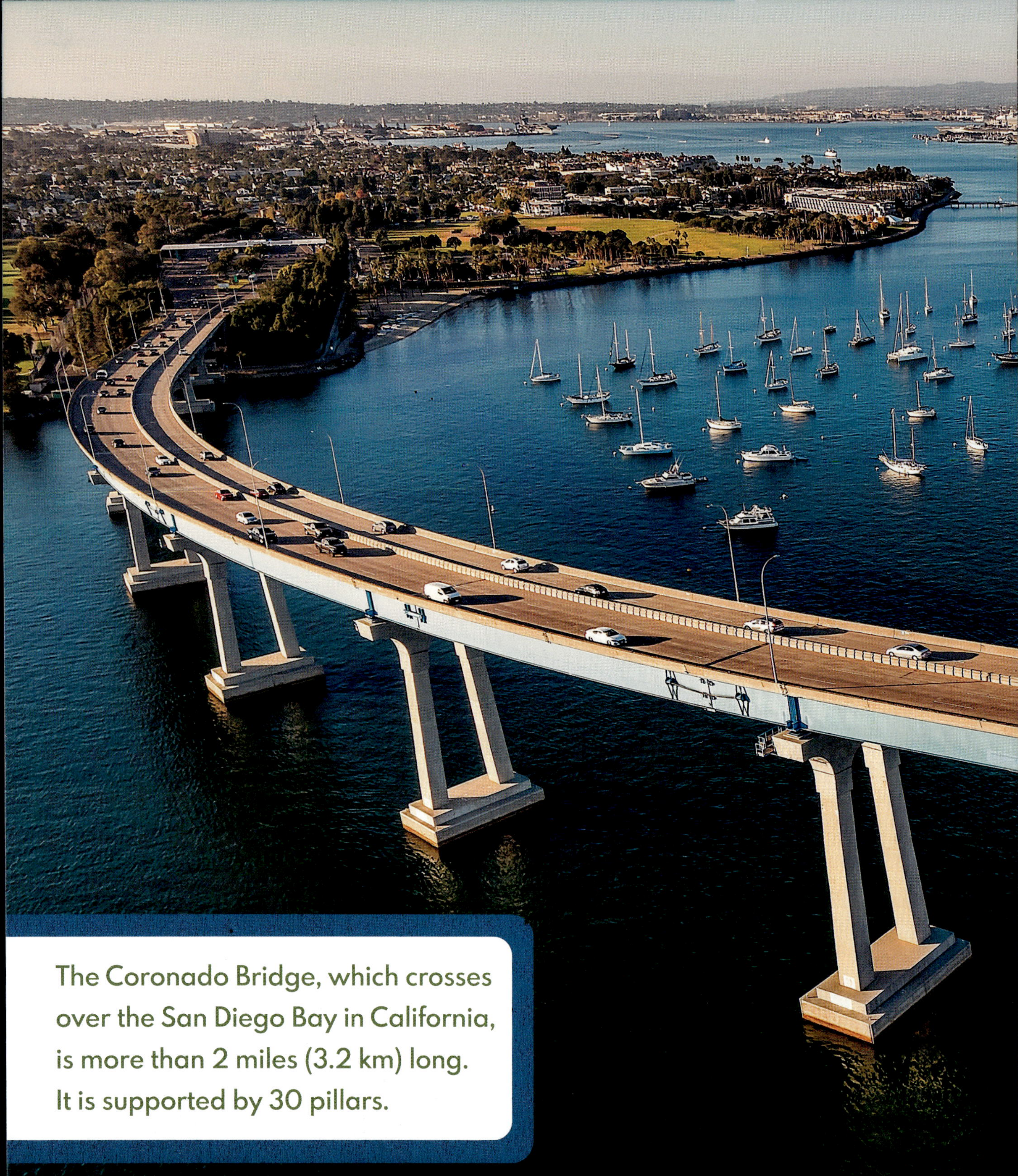

The Coronado Bridge, which crosses over the San Diego Bay in California, is more than 2 miles (3.2 km) long. It is supported by 30 pillars.

CHAPTER 2

Types of Bridges

There are a few kinds of bridges. The simplest type is a beam bridge. A beam bridge is a **horizontal** beam supported on both sides. Weight on the bridge pushes down on the supports. Long beam bridges use posts along the bridge for support.

Strong Shapes

A truss bridge is a stronger form of a beam bridge. Trusses are structures along the sides of a bridge. Each truss has horizontal beams along the bottom and top. Engineers add **diagonal** beams to create a series of triangle shapes.

Triangles are strong. When a **force** presses on a triangle, two sides squeeze together. This is called compression. The third side is

The Longest Bridge

The Danyang–Kunshan Grand Bridge is the longest bridge in the world. The beam bridge crosses Kunshan, China. It is about 100 miles (165 km) long. This bridge allows trains to run through the city. The railway passes over top of many obstacles, such as highways and houses.

There are several types of truss patterns a bridge may use. Each type of truss works the same way but looks a bit different.

pulled outward, creating tension. The tension and compression are equal. Triangles will not lose their shape even under strong forces. The triangle shapes in trusses make the bridge strong enough to support heavy weights, or loads.

Arch bridges also get their strength from their shape. These roadways may pass over or through an arch. Weight on the bridge causes the material of the arch to compress. Compression makes the arch bridge strong.

Suspended by Cables

In a suspension bridge, the roadway hangs from **vertical** cables called suspenders. These suspenders attach to the bridge's main cables. The main cables reach from one end of the bridge to the other. They go over towers that rise above the bridge.

The suspenders pull on the main cables. The main cables and suspenders are all in tension. The main cables push down on the towers,

Forces on a Suspension Bridge

A suspension bridge's towers experience compression. The suspenders and main cables are in tension. These forces help the bridge stay strong.

causing compression in the towers. The forces of compression and tension are equal. They hold the bridge steady.

The Charilaos Trikoupis Bridge is a cable-stayed bridge in Greece. Cables are connected to four towers along the bridge.

On each side of the bridge, the cables are attached to anchorages. These are solid connections to rock or concrete. Load on the bridge is **transferred** through the cables to the anchorages. The connections keep the bridge strong.

Cable-stayed bridges are similar to suspension bridges. But a cable-stayed bridge does not have suspenders. Instead, the roadway hangs from cables that are attached directly to towers along the bridge.

Further Evidence

Look at the website below. Does it give any new evidence to support Chapter Two?

How Does a Suspension Bridge Work?

abdocorelibrary.com/bridges-stand-strong

Workers attached cables while building the Golden Gate Bridge, an iconic suspension bridge in California.

CHAPTER 3

Building a Bridge

Building a bridge takes a long time. The first step is to design the bridge. **Engineers** consider many factors to make sure a new bridge is strong and safe.

Engineers must choose the best type of bridge to use.

The Yangsigang Yangtze River Bridge in China is one of the world's longest suspension bridges. It stretches more than 1 mile (1.7 km).

They consider the length it must span, the forces it will experience, and the surrounding land. Once the bridge is planned, construction may begin.

Length and Load

Bridges span obstacles of different sizes. Some types of bridges are better for small gaps. Others can stay strong even when they are very long. Suspension bridges can be longer than many other bridges. This is because the bridge is supported from above and below.

When Engineering Goes Wrong

The Tacoma Narrows Bridge was a suspension bridge in Washington. It became known as Galloping Gertie because of the dangerous way it twisted in the wind. On November 7, 1940, the bridge collapsed into the water below.

The Garabit Viaduct is an arch bridge in France. The arch is made of curved trusses. The holes in the trusses allow wind to pass through the bridge instead of pushing against it.

Engineers must also think about what forces a bridge will experience. Weather and traffic affect bridges. Arch bridges are good for windy locations. Arch bridges can stay sturdy when wind blows against them. Suspension bridges may sway in the wind. This is dangerous.

All bridges must hold up the weight of the traffic they will carry. Truss bridges are often used for railroad bridges. The extra support of the trusses allows the bridge to hold up heavy trains.

Sturdy Surroundings

Engineers design strong foundations to support bridges. A foundation is an underground structure. The land around a bridge impacts what type of foundation is needed.

If the soil around a bridge is soft, it will need a deep foundation. Workers use piles to support the bridge. Piles are steel or concrete posts that reach deep into the ground to support a structure.

Special machines are used to push piles into the ground. Piles can be used on dry land or in soil under bodies of water.

Special features are needed for a bridge built over water. Caissons are a type of pile. They are underwater structures that create a foundation for a bridge's support posts.

Caissons are built on land. Then they are brought to the river and sunk. They help create a solid foundation for bridges.

Sometimes caissons are hollow. Sometimes they are filled with concrete.

Once piles have been placed, the foundation of a bridge is built. Then the support posts go up. The roadway and any towers are built last.

Engineers continue to design new bridges that can span longer gaps while staying strong. The Millau Viaduct in France is about 1.5 miles (2.4 km) long.

The bridge is tested to make sure it is safe. Finally the bridge is ready for traffic.

Bridges all around the world allow people and vehicles to cross over obstacles. Engineers design these bridges to fit the needs of their locations. Each bridge is built to stay strong while handling force.

Primary Source

Roberto Ballarini is an engineer. He explained that bridges can get weaker over time from the repeated force of traffic. He said:

> If you take a paper clip, and if you bend it once or twice it won't break. However, if you keep repeating that . . . you will [start] cracks, and then the cracks will [spread] and you will actually break the metal into two pieces.

Source: Sea Stachura. "The Big Question." *Minnesota Public Radio News*, 8 Aug. 2007, mprnews.org. Accessed 6 June 2024.

What's the Big Idea?

Read this quote carefully. What is its main idea? Explain how the main idea is supported by details.

Engineering Facts

Truss Bridge

Roadways carry cars, trains, or other traffic.

Trusses use tension and compression to help bridges stand strong.

Arch Bridge

The shape of the arch supports the bridge. Weight compresses the arch.

Suspension Bridge

Towers along the bridge are compressed by the cables.

Cables stretch across the length of a suspension bridge.

Cables are attached to anchorages in solid rock or concrete.

The roadway hangs from suspenders.

Glossary

diagonal
related to a straight line joining two opposite corners of a straight-sided shape

engineer
a person who is trained to design and build machines and structures

force
a push or pull that transfers energy into an object

horizontal
related to a straight line that runs side to side

span
to stretch across

transferred
passed from one thing to another

vertical
related to a straight line that runs up and down

Online Resources

To learn more about bridges, visit our free resource websites below.

Visit **abdocorelibrary.com** or scan this QR code for free Common Core resources for teachers and students, including vetted activities, multimedia, and booklinks, for deeper subject comprehension.

Visit **abdobooklinks.com** or scan this QR code for free additional online weblinks for further learning. These links are routinely monitored and updated to provide the most current information available.

Learn More

Baker, Laura. *Physics for Curious Kids.* Arcturus, 2022.

Olson, Elsie. *Engineering Lab.* Abdo, 2024.

Ventura, Marne. *Why Arches and Triangles Are Strong.* Abdo, 2025.

Index

About the Author

Joanne Mattern is the author of many nonfiction books for children. She especially likes writing about science, nature, and history. Joanne lives in New York State with her family.